Crescendo Publishing Presents

Instant Insights on...

BUSINESS

Taking Your Business from Startup to Thrive in 45 Days

Jodi Masters

small guides. BIG IMPACT.

Instant Insights on...

Taking Your Business from Startup to Thrive in 45 Days
By Jodi Masters

ISBN: 978-1-944177-41-6 (p)
ISBN: 978-1-944177-42-3 (e)

Crescendo Publishing, LLC
300 Carlsbad Village Drive
Ste. 108A, #443
Carlsbad, California 92008-2999

www.CrescendoPublishing.com
GetPublished@CrescendoPublishing.com

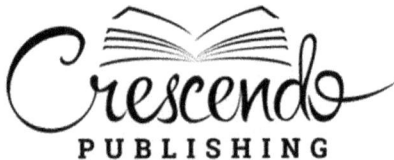

Crescendo
PUBLISHING

What You'll Learn in this Book

In *Taking Your Business from Startup to Thrive in 45 Days*, you'll learn strategies to identify your natural talents and turn them into passionate, successful businesses within forty-five days. Based on her own forty-five-day journey, Jodi Masters breaks down the strategy, identifies perceived problems, and provides viable solutions while incorporating real-life examples along the way. *Taking Your Business from Startup to Thrive in 45 Days* will keep you on track with expert planning, downloadable tools and resources, and an overall strategy for success. Get ready to do what you love and live in your full potential. Let's launch to thrive in forty-five days.

In this book, you'll get **Instant Insights** on...

- Discovering your life's purpose
- Finding a champion
- Making a decision to start
- Manifesting the money
- Manifesting your Dream Team
- Developing your brand elements
- Creating your online digital spaces
- Igniting your digital presence

- Creating a technical infrastructure for growth
- Maintaining your "thrive"

A Gift from the Author

To help you implement the strategies mentioned in this *Instant Insights™* book and get the most value from the content, the author has prepared the following bonus gifts we know you will love:

- *Access to the Audio Book Version*
- *45-Day Plan Template*
- *Copy of My Own 45-Day Plan*
- *My Dream Team Directory*
- *Software Recommendations*

You can get instant access to these complimentary materials here:
www.webvoice.com/StartUpToThrive

Table of Contents

Dedication

To my son Frankie, the light of my life.

To my mother, my first champion.

To Mr. Adam Leipzig, my virtual champion.

To Angela Moore, the best wing-woman ever.

And last but not least to Teri Black, who shined a spotlight on me in her limelight, and shot me out of a cannon.

Discovering Your Life's Purpose (or Natural Talents) in 5 Minutes

I am Jodi, and I invent digital business opportunities for entrepreneurs. I show them specific ways to leverage the Internet to create digital versions of their product and services. As a result, they transform into more confident, successful entrepreneurs, thriving in their full potential.

The most common problem I see with my entrepreneurial clients is they either do not know their natural talents, or they do not believe they can be successful in them. They are often at a point where their restlessness and discontent are finally pushing them to jump off a cliff into the free-fall of "their own thing," but they don't know exactly how or where to start. Many reach this point because they find themselves squarely in a life transition and/or in a J.O.B. that isn't their passion—it's work, it's stressful, and they will poke their eyes out if they continue to do it for another second.

If you feel strongly that you have already uncovered your life's purpose, feel free to skip ahead to the next chapter. However, if you have the slightest doubt, or simply want to reaffirm what you already believe, then I encourage you to keep reading with an open mind for a new experience of yourself, your natural talents, and how you make people feel because of what you do.

Finding myself nearly paralyzed in this dilemma and praying for a sign, I got what I asked for. I was online and saw a TEDx talk with the headline *"Discover Your Life's Purpose in 5 Minutes."*

You can view the talk here:

https://youtu.be/vVsXO9brK7M

The timing of it was so spot-on I couldn't believe it. If I've said it once, I've said it a million times: be careful what you ask for! I thought, "After all this time, is this guy really gonna tell me in a video what my life's purpose is?" Something key happened in that moment: *I became willing to be coachable.* I clicked play and watched the video with an open mind, willing to see myself through a new lens.

In his amazing TEDx talk (which I am not being paid in any way to promote), author, filmmaker, and educator, Adam Leipzig speaks about his experience of developing his simple five-minute process of self-discovery. It came after attending his twenty-five-year Yale reunion, where about only 20 percent of his graduating class said they were happy in their lives. The "happy" Yale grads knew the following five things about themselves:

- Who they were
- What they did
- Who they did it for
- What those people wanted or needed
- How those people changed as a result

Pause. Try it now. Write it down. Take it in.

Like many people who go through Leipzig process, and as sure as the sun will rise in the morning, I knew what I had written was right on: I was an expert in my natural talent, and it could be developed into my passion.

Problem #2: I had to figure out how to convert my natural talent and expert training into a passion. I discovered the solution was twofold: I needed to get very specific about the area of my unique qualification that I *loved* and who I most enjoyed spending my time with, specifically my ideal client. Solving these two riddles enabled me to begin manifesting a deep passion for my work and the people I was working with. Yes, you too can love your work, the people you work with, and your clients! This was the wind that blew me over the edge into my latest entrepreneurial freefall and enabled me to give it 100 percent of my time and resources. I eliminated all Plan Bs and focused solely on my Plan A.

What was my process of solving Problem #2? I went back to Mr. Leipzig's last three questions.

- Who they did it for
- What those people wanted or needed
- How those people changed as a result

Who they did it for is your ideal client. When I thought about my ideal client, a couple specific clients came to mind. As a result, I was able to define characteristics about them, such as:

- Their basic demographics: gender, age, marital status, children, level of education, profession, and industry
- Where they spend time online *and* offline
- The level of customer service required to make them feel special

What those people wanted or needed are the services I needed to focus on providing. Here is where I found the real connection. The specific services or products my ideal clients continue to buy from me are what keeps us connected *and* creates a positive change for them.

How those people changed as a result is my fuel. It makes me feel so full and fulfilled when my ideal clients change as a result of my services. It doesn't have to be a huge change in the way you or I would measure change; it just has to be a change that the client feels in some measure that keeps them coming back to you. One of my ideal clients told me I was instrumental in helping her achieve her million-dollar annual gross revenue goal. Another client told me he didn't know he needed me until we helped them with their key messaging while performing a website redesign and strategic social media campaign. I don't judge what constitutes change or how they define success. As long as the client feels it, they will sing your praises and keep coming back.

Mr. Leipzig's "bonus" question literally transforms into your elevator pitch and delivers you firmly into Day 1 of your forty-five-day plan of launching or growing your business. You must practice it, refine it, live it, breath it. (If you haven't watched his video yet, do it now!)

Here's mine:

I am Jodi, and I help entrepreneurs thrive in their full potential. (Then people ask me *how*, and the conversation starts.)

Your Instant Insights...

- Watch Mr. Leipzig's TEDx video and explore your life's purpose using his five-question process.

- Explore your life's purpose with an open mind using Mr. Leipzig's five-question process.

- Embody your elevator pitch, and yell it from the rooftops.

Find Your Champions

Now that you've discovered your life's purpose, it's time to find your champions. These people are key as you set out on this journey. They are essential in helping you create and maintain a powerful, bionic atmosphere. When doubt, vulnerability, and negative people infiltrate, your champions will be your army who will continuously shine light on your path. It's your job to find them and give them a lantern.

Problem #1: Where do you find your champions? More than likely, you have a few key champions in your life already. You can spot them because they are the ones who are usually excited and happy to see you. They already know how you make them feel when you spend time together (which is positive!).

The first champion I "found" turned out to be one of my existing clients. I valued our relationship greatly but hadn't yet realized how much she valued me. During one of our meetings, I shared that I had made the decision to rebrand and relaunch my business. She immediately replied, "I've been waiting for you to say that! I can't WAIT to see what you do. I know it'll be something big!"

It's incredible how much power she gave me in that moment. She filled my tank with jet fuel that lasted my own forty-five days. She already believed in me, just like I already believe in you. (Let's have some fun and send her some virtual love @teriblack. C'mon, send her a tweet right now that says "World's Best Champion!")

Solution #1:
Ask your favorite and ideal clients the last question in Leipzig Process, "How do people change as a result of what I do?" Rephrase it so that it makes sense in your situation. Remember the key aspect here is *the action of asking*. This signals your willingness to be open for a new experience of yourself. Don't be shy about asking follow-up questions too.

Solution #2:
Ask family, friends, your church community, and/ or people who are engaged in your hobbies (sports, running, writing, art, etc.), who are happy and excited to spend time with you, the same question.

You may feel weird, vulnerable, or awkward doing this. Do it anyway. Even if you receive seemingly insignificant responses like "because your smile lights up the room," these too will add up and begin to have an incredible effect on you.

Solution #3:
Are you having trouble finding people who are happy and excited to spend time with you? Are you getting feedback that feels like criticism or the weight of a million bags of sand? You are either asking the wrong people (remember to ask those who are *happy and excited* to spend time with you), or *you* may lack being of service to other people. In our bonus gift, we have a number of people under Chapter 2 of the Dream Team Directory who can help you sort this one out.

So let's break it down in another example:

Another one of my champion clients turned out to be within my church network. Although I've known him and his family for some time, I'd say he was more an acquaintance than somebody I knew well.

I happened to be in his office one day and overheard him speaking to his chief marketing officer about needing to redesign his website. He's an equity lender in a very competitive marketplace. Because my radar is up at all times, looking for ideal clients and champions, I seized the opportunity to share with him my expertise in leveraging the Internet to invent digital opportunities for entrepreneurs. This led to a short conversation about their Internet marketing strategy, what they needed to get out of the investment, and how their website fits within that framework. His CMO asked for a proposal on the spot.

I saw an opportunity and took action. I shared with him my Leipzig pitch (from the first chapter), which led to the opportunity.

We had cash in hand within the week to start the project and finished the project on time, with a little extra service thrown in.

I was in service to this client with a generous, grateful attitude.

To this day, he tells the story that he didn't know he needed me before he knew my expertise, which is why we need to share with everyone, from Day 1, our Leipzig pitch.

He shares with people that he's had a number of potential clients who decided to hire him after visiting his website because they saw faces they recognized from the community, along with their testimonials, which made them feel safe about hiring him.

The service I provided him changed his perception of the power of the Internet and opened up growth opportunities for his business he didn't know existed. This enabled him to convert undecided clients in a way he wasn't able to before, which had an immediate positive impact on his bottom line. He's transformed from ideal client into a champion.

Champions rise up from our entire network: existing clients, new clients, our community, our friends, our family, and even people we pay to help us grow. I have the best therapist in the whole wide world (who is also listed in our Dream Team Directory). I also hired a business coach. I meet with people every week specifically for spiritual fellowship; this helps so much with faith and forging ahead into the unknown. Champions may live in virtual space too, like Mr. Leipzig, whose video inspired me (in less than five minutes I might add), to thrive in my full potential. A slice of which is sharing my experience with you...now.

Remember, if it was easy, everyone would do it. Go get it!

Your Instant Insights...

- Share your Leipzig pitch with everyone, every day.

- Ask the people in your network who enjoy spending time with you the appropriate version of, "How do people change as a result of what I do?"

- Remain vigilantly connected to your champions, being proactive in reaching out to them if negative people or feelings infiltrate.

Make a Decision to Start

Now that you've discovered your talents and found your champions, there are only two things left to do: make a decision to start and *then start*!

Throughout my life, I've always tended to work on multiple businesses at the same time. I eventually realized that by doing that, rarely did I do any of them to my full potential. I found that *not* having a backup plan was essential to my being successful in business. Setting yourself up for success is critical to launching your new business in forty-five days.

Remember that if you're giving attention to Plan B, then you're not giving 100 percent of your attention to Plan A.

My decision to relaunch Webvoice, Inc. happened without a lot of fanfare. I simply made up my mind to do it—to do it in forty-five days as a super-special goal—then reaffirmed to myself that I could do almost anything for forty-five days if I just focused on one day at a time. So I made a big-picture plan, then worked my plan, day after day. I started on February 1 (my birthday), which meant my launch was March 15.

Are you ready to start?
Are you willing to give it 100 percent of your time, resources, and energy?

If so, kiss and hug your loved ones good-bye. You'll be back soon!

Day 1 date: _____ Welcome to Day 1!
Day 45 date: _____ Your official launch date. Whoop!

Congratulations! Looking back, I found making the decision was the hardest part. I felt so vulnerable and excited in that moment. I *never* needed to give 100 percent before; 20 to 30 percent power was usually good enough to comfortably meet my basic needs. I was so curious to finally know my full potential self for the first time. Onward!

Step One: Create Instant Accountability.

- Call and tell as many champions as possible about your decision. You will probably feel very vulnerable and exposed. They got you on this.

- Begin telling everyone you speak with every day that you are in the process of launching your business, and that your launch date is _____.

- Post your decision, launch date, and your Leipzig pitch on all your social networks ...

- ... and let me know about it @webvoice and #StartUpToThrive!

- Practice your elevator pitch on everyone you meet. As you do this, you will discover that people naturally ask more, *which is the goal.* They become an opportunity to be a champion and/or client in that moment!

Step Two: Create a 45-Day Plan

(In our bonus gift, we have a forty-five-day template for you to use to design your own forty-five-day plan. Also included is the forty-five-day plan that I created when we relaunched Webvoice, Inc.)

What does a forty-five-day startup plan look like?

For me, it was not linear. I didn't do chapter one, then two, then three, and so on, one after another, the first, then the next, until it was all done. The reality is once you read this book and examine our forty-five-day plan template, you'll see that many of the suggested activities will overlap.

What are the actions of a forty-five-day plan?

This book is a road map through what I found to be the most essential actions as I was re-launching Webvoice, Inc. They include:

- Manifesting your money (your current clients and champions are key players in this one)
- Assembling your Dream Team
- Developing your brand elements
- Creating your online spaces and networks
- Igniting your digital business
- Creating a technical infrastructure for growth
- Maintaining your thrive

Print out the template, get out a pen, and map out your forty-five-day plan. Note that you will work on many of these actions concurrently over the approximate six-week period. Remaining fluid, as the process ebbs and flows, is really important. Make sure to interact with your champions a few times each week. Make lunch dates with them to be efficient—fill your cup while you eat!

Step Three: Envision What "Launching" Looks like for You

We have this idea that launching our business means having a perfectly wrapped package on Day 45. The truth is it will be perfect because it's not finished yet. It is only the beginning.

When I envisioned relaunching Webvoice, Inc., I saw a core team and a basic operational infrastructure in place, plus my first few *new* clients. To me, this meant the business was bringing in money and signaled viability. Making an online splash on my "launch" day made it real. But you know what? It was very modest. I ended up doing a simple but effective two-page website. We opted for an animated infographic, an interactive storytelling tool with which to engage the client.

It made our website unique while we shared our Leipzig pitch with our target demographic—the story of who we are, who our clients are, the various services we provide, and the change they receive as a result of working with us. It ends with a button call that says *Start Now,* which links to a contact form. On March 15, 2016, I announced the relaunch of Webvoice, Inc. in my digital spaces and networks. And that was it. Then a flood of comments, likes, and energy flowed forward; it was very exciting and reaffirming. That is what relaunching Webvoice, Inc. meant for me.

Your Instant Insights...

- Make the decision to start and dedicate all your energy, resources, and time to your Plan A for the next forty-five days.

- Create accountability by telling everyone about your Leipzig pitch and your launch date. Post it on all your social media platforms.

- Create your forty-five-day plan and decide what launching looks like for you.

Manifesting the Money: Your First Clients and Evangelists

We all have the power to manifest money for the starting of our business beginning Day 1. We begin this process by telling everyone we meet about what we do and the change they will receive as a result of working with us. Our Leipzig pitch leads to a conversation about our work and value, which leads to the opportunity, a proposal, then hopefully new business.

If you are a people person, you're going to love this next part of the forty-five-day journey. If not, then you will really transform in this chapter by getting out of your comfort zone.

Time is money, and money likes speed.

So why forty-five days and who are these evangelists? I saw a forty-five-day goal as a two-for-one: I needed to maximize the investment into the relaunch of Webvoice, Inc., and I needed to maximize the value my new clients received from me. The faster I could get to market, the faster my business would be legitimized, which leads to a greater amount of credibility, which leads to buying confidence. The faster I get my projects done, the faster my clients can also generate heightened buying confidence, which leads them to sing my prai$e$. Bang, my evangelists—client champions who become your referring workforce—are born.

Turning your first clients into evangelists.

How do you convert your evangelists into a referring workforce? You do so by being very specific about who you'd like referrals to. Each week you can ask for another variation or person. Give your evangelists as much specificity as possible:

- Ideal profile of ideal client: specific name, title, and company name of a lead you want to be introduced to; for example, *Jane Smith, CEO, bizbang.com*

- A title, company type, and geographic area; for example, *CEO or executive at dentist offices in the South Bay*
- Describe a need or challenge your ideal client might have: for example, *Entrepreneurs or CEOs who strongly dislike their website or who think Internet marketing does not work for them*
- Something less specific (and less effective) like *entrepreneurs or CEOs wanting to start or grow their business*

Obviously, the more specific you can get, the better. You can also use this technique when "asking" for any need your startup or growing business might have, including referrals to experts or when searching for your ideal team members. You will find that adding capacity can have its own set of challenges that your network can help with as well.

This is how you convert your client champions into your evangelists, waiting for the opportunity to refer business to you. Your non-client champions will also work for you in the same way, but your client champions are special because they've received firsthand value, an emotional experience, as a direct result from working with you.

Developing Other Types of Evangelists

Start tapping into your all your networks and scheduling meetings with everyone in them. Of particular value are business networking groups. In our Dream Team Directory (in your bonus gift) we have a list of superb business networking groups with whom we've had a tremendous amount of success.

So smile and dial, baby! Schedule as many meetings as you can—by phone and in person— and start the meeting with your pitch. During those meetings, you will find that your pitch will flow into a conversation about your products or services and the value you bring to your clients.

Fishing vs. Farming

I saw every meeting I scheduled as a lead and evangelist opportunity. In the really good business networking groups, most of the CEOs really understand this principle. The biggest value comes from figuring out how you can develop this person into someone who will refer you a lot of business. The answer is to be that person too. Become a referring machine. Be of service to your CEO and entrepreneurial peers, and they will reward you in kind. By doing this, you are creating new champions and evangelists.

You might have heard the phrase "fishing or farming" in sales strategy conversations.

Developing your networks would be an example of *farming.* You are planting seeds that, if nurtured, will bear you fruit in a very short period of time. Be patient with this process.

And then there is fishing. This is when you cast your net, hook a fish, and eat it for dinner that night. In some cases you will find the right customer at precisely the right time because you are out there sharing your pitch with everyone you meet. When lightning strikes, the most essential key is to make sure you respond to that client immediately. You must give them a quote immediately and follow up with them immediately. Do not make them wait twenty-four hours; respond to them within hours.

As you begin to start this process of manifesting money, you may feel a little panic (I did anyway). You may find yourself questioning if the money will come in fast enough. You've set your forty-five-day goal, told everyone about it, and now you're waiting for the pieces to start clicking into place. Whenever that fear or doubt infiltrates, reach out to your champions for a reminder of why they're your champions, and get back to the plan.

Your Instant Insights...

- Turn your first clients into evangelists by asking them for a specific kind of referral at every opportunity. Redefine your ask at regular intervals.

- Be of service to your CEO/ entrepreneurial peers by becoming a referring machine for them too – you'll get it back 10x

- Understand the concepts of "fishing" vs. "farming." Be patient and nurture your fields. They are a very valuable crop. You can't fish in an empty pond.

Manifesting Your Dream Team

Being able to delegate is so fundamental to business growth. It is impossible to grow or get through launching your business in forty-five days without the help of others.

What are the qualities of a Dream Team?

After I assembled my Dream Team, I noticed they had the following traits in common:

- They have a team mentality and were willing to be flexible to the needs of the company *first*.

- Timing was key when I found them; they had all *just* become available.

- They were all trainable and coachable.
- I enjoyed working with each of them. They smile, laugh, and love what they do.
- They are natural problem solvers and are very resourceful.
- They naturally see the glass half-full.
- They speak and write English very well.

I learned very quickly that:

- Working remotely could be very advantageous because you have a bigger pool of opportunities, and as a result, you will require less office (or no office) space.
- I did not have time to mess around with people who are not actually available to get the work done, are flakey, or have conflicting priorities.
- Cheaper is not an advantage. The advantage is *capacity*, which means we can turn around our projects in a short time frame, with a very high level of quality.
- As far as "experts" or "coaches" go, if I was not getting what I needed from them, I would find a replacement. Just because someone is a subject-matter expert doesn't mean they automatically have the capacity to give you what you need, or that they match your "Dream Team" qualities above.

Where to Find a Dream Team?

The solution is similar to where you find your champions—they are more than likely already around you in your existing networks. Begin asking for your Dream Team members every day; ask for specific referrals (be as descriptive as possible in the same way you should be asking for your ideal client). Ask in posts on your social networks, in your e-zine, or on your blog. The more you speak about and ask for them, the more frequently possibilities will begin to appear.

The first person I hired when I relaunched Webvoice, Inc. was Lauren, my Manager of Client Relations. Lauren came to me around Day 21 of our relaunch. I was concentrating so hard on finding her that when a local cycling studio announced they were suddenly closing, I immediately wondered whether their fabulous front-office woman had found another job yet. So I called and left her a message, and she returned my call *that day*. Lauren *always* met me with a big smile. She *always* knew my name. She *always* helped me select the best package for my needs. I knew she'd pick up on our system because she learned the studio's overly complicated web-based system (not naming names), so I knew she was smart and could learn. More than anything, as a client, she made me feel special. Sound familiar?

Building Elastic Capacity

I learned early on in my work that my clients' needs can vary greatly. When it comes to my creative team, I need to have a kind of capacity that could expand and contract as needed. For example, one graphic designer could not meet *all* the style needs of *all* my clients. I needed a way to flex the skill set and size of my team on short notice, depending on my work flow. Having elastic capacity also enabled me to have very manageable overhead costs.

Second-Most Important Team Member: A Sourcerer

I began realizing that a lot of my time and focus was being spent on *sourcing* my team. I needed to find a way to do this more effectively—finding more qualified people, but taking less of my time to do so. I needed to delegate to a sourcerer.

As it turns out, a wonderful young woman in my network named Iman was just the gal. I wanted her so badly to join my Dream Team, but she was already in love with another. However, she knew a lot of freelancers who were really good because that was part of her existing job responsibilities. She began sending me the best referrals for all the specific people I asked for. I pay her very well by the hour to do this occasional but magical work for me.

Building Your Dream Team

Whenever I find a great person, even if I can't hire them right then and there, I add them to my Dream Team Directory as a future possibility. My Dream Team Directory is a special list of people who provide exceptional value in their services. I use this list in a variety of ways:

- To enable me to be a very reliable, effective referring machine (the "you get what you give mentality")
- To meet the needs of my clients or CEO/ entrepreneurial peers when *they are seeking* a Dream Team member
- As a way of anticipating my own future needs, always fishing and farming wonderful people to work with
- Ensuring my elastic capacity

Great team members are very hard to come by, so whenever you find someone fabulous, treat them like any great opportunity and put them in your pipe! Recruiting should be an ongoing process.

Not too long ago, a champion client had been looking for a business manager for over six months. Frustrated, she began asking everyone she spoke with about her need, specifically asking for the qualifications and qualities of the person she was looking for. Because *I'm also her champion*, I automatically began keeping her need in mind as I was out doing my days. Within a short period of time, I realized one of my very best friends was an ideal candidate for her and orchestrated a love connection.

As I took on the project of writing this book, I became overwhelmed by the discipline it would take to block out huge parts of the day to get it done. I felt like it would be a lot easier if I could dictate my chapters and have someone transcribe them for me, effectively creating a first draft. So I started speaking about this need, and within approximately twenty-four hours I found someone—Angela, my wingwoman. She's like a writing trainer. We created a schedule, and she was there every day with me, producing the transcripts to help me accomplish this goal. Because of her, I was able to write this book ... in ten days!

Your Instant Insights...

- Define the qualities of your Dream Team.
- Don't be cheap; think of CAPACITY!
- Immediately cut loose anyone who is not meeting your needs.

Developing Your Brand Elements

Developing your brand elements is an extension of everything we've discussed so far. Your branding will present itself to the outside world at various touch points—in your e-mails, during meetings with potential clients and vendors, in your corporate culture, and through all your marketing collateral, including all your digital spaces and website.

Why is branding so important?

Branding elements include aspects you are probably already familiar with, such as your logo and the overall look and feel of your marketing pieces. Branding also includes all aspects of your messaging. This includes all the written words or copy used to describe you, your company, and your goods and services. It also includes the visual images you use to convey emotion, including humor or inspiration, in your choice of photography and video. Brand messaging is also conveyed via your company culture, your philosophy, your community connection, and your integrity.

People get to know your brand on all levels of its interaction with the outside world. When it's authentic, the outside world feels it—*for better or for worse.*

Developing Your Brand Elements

So where's the starting point?

When we work with clients, we *always* start with (surprise!) the Leipzig process of developing key messaging. Go back and review yours. Write it here:

_____

_____

_____

_____

_____

Client-centered messaging

_____

_____

_____

_____

Focusing on the value or the change your client receives as a result of your services, it is necessary to conceptualize what it looks like and sounds like <u>*from the emotional side of your client's experience with you.*</u>

A very functional benefit of asking your clients about the value or the change they receive as a result of working with you is that you begin to develop a *listening muscle* for the positive emotional experience your clients experience as a result of your services.

This is what I call *client-centric* or *client-centered messaging.* Instead of focusing on *you*, focus instead on the challenges, problems, and/or needs of your typical ideal client.

Finding Your Branding Dream Team

When we work with clients to develop their strategic key messaging and branding elements, we work with a Dream Team of creative professionals to bring it all to life. First and foremost, however, we start here:

- Develop an overall key messaging strategy focused on the client experience.

- Examine all of the client's existing marketing collateral, including their logo, copy, social media content, and all photography and video. We also study their company culture and values. Does it all line up?

- We redesign the pieces that need a makeover from a messaging point of view. Nine times out of ten, it's the key messaging that's broken. For some reason, people in this country are severely focused on highlighting themselves in their marketing, often neglecting the emotional connection to their ideal client. *Successful companies know this connection is the secret marketing sauce.*

- We make sure the client stands out from the competition. Big secret: it's usually not that hard because the competition is a competition of lookalikes. When you focus on your clients, you are already doing something *very different.*

When you look at all your strategic key messaging, what is it saying? Does it have a unified identity, or does it look schizophrenic? Do all your branding elements share a common style and message? Who does your messaging speak about most?

Key Branding Elements

Let's dive deeper into each brand element. Your startup branding elements should typically include the following:

- *Your strategic key messaging.* This is the work we did in chapter 1. Many of my clients come to me when they feel their website or social marketing is broken in some way. They think they need a brand-new website to address these issues, but in most cases, it's their strategic key messaging that needs to be fixed.

- *Your logo.* This is where most people begin when branding their business. We try to incorporate symbolically the point of confluence between the change my client's customer receives as a result of working with her, and my client's identity as an entrepreneur. What might that symbol look like for you?

- *Your copy.* Copy includes all words used to market your business. It may be your bio, descriptions of your products or services, and/or any description in a brochure or on your website—even the 140 characters you use in tweets on Twitter.

- *Your images and video.* These elements are a micro study into your strategic key messaging on a visual frequency. Do the images you use convey the client's emotional connection with your products or services, or are your images all about you? Don't freak out—you are not alone. You just need a team to help you get it on track.

Don't forget the seasoning your company culture adds to your branding. When you and all your competitors are lined up, how do you stand out? Sometimes the key differentiator is your company culture. You and your team are an essential part of your company brand. Does your client feel they can identify with you, your employees, and your culture? Is it relaxed? Do they feel at ease working with you? That also extends to the quality of your products and services, as well as your customer service. How quickly are you responding? Do you have a can-do attitude?

Your Instant Insights...

- Develop your brand elements. Realize that it's a process, not a one-and-done.
- Create client-centered strategic messaging.
- Realize that the outside world will perceive your brand on all levels. No matter how pretty it is, if it's not authentic, they'll know it.

Creating Your Online Spaces

A digital presence, above and beyond your website, is absolutely essential for doing business today. However, it's not a one size fits all. Company needs vary in a variety of ways, including where their target demographics or ideal clients spend time online. Digital Internet spaces, when leveraged correctly, have a fantastic opportunity to provide all kinds of support for your brand, including building brand awareness, building your brand popularity and networks, and creating or enhancing credibility, which all lead to a more confident buying experience for your client—when done right.

How to Know What You Really Need

These days a website is considered a standard, essential business need, but buzzword services such as social media or SEO *may not be*. Are services like SEO still necessary? How do you determine what you really need and those you don't?

There is No One-Size-Fits-All Solution

Every company is unique, so beware of companies who try to sell you a "package." Ask about each element, then ask yourself, is this where my ideal client is spending time? Is this element something that will help create credibility with my target demographic? Will my ideal client look for me, or is she more likely to buy from me because I show up in her online space? Not sure? Survey your audience! Actually asking your ideal clients these questions on a regular basis helps you stay on top of shifting trends.

In my experience, the following digital spaces seem to be fairly standard for most businesses these days:

- *A great website* that tells the story of who you are, who your ideal client is, the products/services you provide, the products or services they think they are buying from you, and the solution or change they receive as a result of working with you. A very simple website is okay if you cover these bases. A call to action (e.g., "call us" or "start now") is essential, along with very visible contact information.

- For locally based businesses, "local" services such as Google places, Yelp, and/or Meetup are very helpful for building brand networks and customer confidence.

- LinkedIn, Facebook, Twitter, and/or Instagram are helpful, depending on the age and interest of your target demographic.

- Other digital spaces, such as blogs, e-zines, webinars, digital books, YouTube channels, or other lead-generating techniques may or may not be a priority. Usually these can be secondary.

Launch Where Your Clients Spend Time Online

It is just as important, if not more so, *to launch where your clients spend time online* rather than sitting back and waiting for them to search for you. Sometimes the appropriate solution is a combination of both. Would they prefer to receive an e-mail from you from time to time? Always ask your customers first. They are the experts on themselves!

Internet spaces focused on *local geographic areas* can be hugely important, depending on your business. For some clients, I may prioritize these sites over the standard Facebook, Twitter, Instagram, and LinkedIn spaces. These include sites and services such as Next Door, Yelp!, Google places, and networks such as Meetup.com. Facebook business pages are great, but they're not as powerful as Facebook groups can be.

The Importance of Reviews and Recommendations

Another consideration to incorporate into your operations is a process of asking for a positive review or recommendation at the conclusion of every project *while the client is feeling the emotional connection* to the solution or change they received as a result of your product or services. The best reviews are made in the afterglow moments!

Great client testimonials are gold and go a long way in creating credibility and buying confidence.

Avoid Bait-and-Switch or Hook Tactics

Bait-and-switch is the tactic of leading your customer to feel connected or special, *for the purpose of selling them something,* rather than for genuine appreciation. Hook tactics are designed to make your clients click for substantive material, but too often very little substance is actually there. Again, they feel you hooked them with the primary purpose of selling them something, rather than actually being of service and providing valuable content.

Ask yourself how do you like these tactics? Ask your clients how they feel about them too. I do believe in responsible, thoughtful nurturing, which can be automated. Just be careful about being blinded by the numbers. Remember, quality over quantity. We want clients who are coming to us happy and excited, not feeling tricked or suspicious!

Your Instant Insights...

- Design and launch a website that engages your potential client with an emotional connection; one that conveys you have what they need (i.e., a solution!).

- Prioritize creating the digital spaces and networks where your clients spend time.

- Avoid bait-and-switch and hook marketing tactics. Be responsible with nurture market-ing strategies, spam sucks!

Igniting Your Business in the Digital Universe (a.k.a. the Internet)

Most of us do not fully understand the different types of social engagement and the full impact it can have on our business, both positive and negative. As a result, it's easy to be lured by expensive marketing services that promise all kinds of incredible "ranking" and results.

The Four Main Types of Social Engagement

Before making a splash in the virtual Internet pond, center yourself again in your goals of your Internet marketing strategy. Is it your goal to create social engagement with your target demographic or ideal client in the online spaces where they spend the most time? Or is it your goal to elevate your level of credibility in the eyes of your ideal clients?

Let's review the four main types of social engagement and prioritize each one for your launch.

- *The first type of social engagement focuses on leads and selling* and goes back to the practice of fishing for clients. To do this, you need to immediately engage with your target demographic in their digital spaces. Being able to launch and immediately start selling often requires a great deal of coordination and commitment of time and dollars. You'll need to hit it hard the moment you launch. If you have weak or small online networks, there won't be much fish to catch organically.

- *The second type of social engagement focuses on networking.* We lovingly refer to this as "virtual farming." This is a process of going into the social spaces and networks where your ideal clients spend time, connecting with them, investing in engagement with them, and cultivating virtual relationships with them. This helps you create a bigger pond to fish in *organically.*

- The best place to start this endeavor is with existing customers, champions, and personal contacts who may or may not be current customers. Invite every single customer you've ever had to network with you online in your social spaces. They are your low-hanging fruit, which means they already know you and love you. These are the people who are also ideal to connect with in the early stages of manifesting money! Reconnect with them and let them know what you're up to.

- *This next type of social engagement is about influencing and building credibility.* Building influence comes in part from aligning with other influencers in your field. As you begin to develop your networks, focusing on influencer relationships can sometimes be powerful because you can receive an immediate boost in credibility by the association. Another valuable aspect to this is teaming with influencers on joint projects.

- *This brings us to the last point of social engagement, listening and interacting.* This needs to happen concurrently with all other efforts, in a committed and ongoing manner, *forever more.* This is a great opportunity to make your ideal clients feel special, and it is where the real magic of social engagement begins.

Prioritizing Your Social Engagement Strategy

Now that you understand each type of social engagement, it's time to prioritize them and focus on igniting your business online. You may be able to effectively do all of these social engagements at once, but depending on your time and budget, you may need to set priorities.

Launching Your Website

Your website is your home base, where you will be driving people to generate leads and turn them into opportunities, which hopefully includes capturing critical client information, and possibly even converting them to client status immediately (i.e., making a sale). This is why your website should be completed early in this process. As we discussed previously, it does not have to be complex.

Conduct a soft launch of your website to work out the kinks before you make your official "splash." This means launching it without announcement while inviting your champions and trusted friends to have a look around and provide feedback. Do the forms work, does it make sense, does it flow, is it appealing? Be sure to ask them what they love and don't love about it. This is really important information.

Launching Your First Digital Campaign

Next, it's time to launch your first digital campaign. We developed our website and our initial social media elements concurrently, so all the pieces came up at the same time. (Check out our #entrepreneursplaylist if you haven't done so already.)

Wait For It ... Launch Patience Really is a Virtue

It's tempting to want to share content prematurely, but we recommend making sure that all your digital spaces align in your key messaging *before* launching, even if elements of your digital marketing plan are ready and waiting.

I decided to launch with a campaign about our client-centered process and how our process solves growth problems and delivers our clients squarely into a thriving digital presence. We decided to write a book about the value of our process to our clients to show proof of concepts. Writing a book is a great way to instantly elevate credibility and build buyer confidence (not to mention, it's a huge accomplishment!). Ask us how we did it in ten days.

You may build engagement and credibility in other ways too, such as a campaign centered completely around your customer's experience. This may include a series of customer testimonials about the changes or solutions they received as a result of your products or services, which is really easy to implement straightaway.

Call your champions for feedback and confirmation if doubts infiltrate, then press the launch button!

Your Instant Insights...

- Review and learn the four main types of social engagement: leads and selling; networking; influencing and building credibility; and listening and interacting.

- Prioritize the social engagement types that make the most sense for your business at the time of launch.

- Invite all your champions to have a look and give you feedback. Listen to them if they all say the same thing!

Creating a Technical Infrastructure for Growth

As your business begins to spin up, you will have a large number of moving parts. So in addition to your Dream Team to whom you delegate, it now becomes essential to implement the right technology to increase organizational capacity and efficiency.

Finding and Choosing the Right Technology

The right technology will not only keep you organized and on track, but it may also help keep you sane!

1. ***Bookkeeping software.*** The first application software I purchased was for bookkeeping and accounting. I opted for an

online version, which I highly recommend because it makes it possible for your entire team to collaborate. My bookkeeper and accountant are able to work remotely, which gives me lots of space and flexibility. I always have access to my books as long as I have Internet access!

2. ***Client relationship management software (or CRM).*** A CRM solution is absolutely essential for tracking your sales pipeline. A CRM system enables you to know exactly when you last communicated with clients, help you identify opportunities and leads, as well as where you have drop-offs (or loss of interest.) Being able to track this information enables you to swiftly address any problems or roadblocks that may be keeping you from converting leads to opportunities, and closing new business.

3. ***Project management software.*** As you take on new projects and clients, there will be more and more pieces to manage, so project management software is a must. This is the best way to effectively manage your client commitments. This software enables you to store all tasks in one location and assign them to your team members, which enables you to effectively progress your projects on schedule.

Being able to see workflow and measure support capacity in your organization is important for making decisions about when to add more support and for managing customer service. Monitoring how the team is progressing on projects also enables you to identify any potential delays and address them immediately.

4. *Time tracking.* Another valuable tool within project management is time tracking. At Webvoice, it enables us to keep track of team-member time and compare estimated hours with actual hours, which is very important for measuring our estimate accuracy and project profitability.

5. *Social media content management and scheduling software.* This software is essential for running social media campaigns because you want to be scheduling content at optimal intervals and be able to see how well your ideal clients engage with this content. This content, beyond promotional messaging, may include inspirational content; technical content that leads to credibility, such as blogs; or reposting and sharing of articles or other kinds of freebies and useful information designed to connect and bond with your ideal client!

6. *Mass e-mailing software* enables you to regularly keep in touch with your leads, opportunities, and clients. The analytics piece helps you see how effective your messages are. You can track how your e-mail campaigns are being received, if they are being automatically marked as spam, and if people are responding positively by opening, forwarding, or clicking through.

7. This last one may not be applicable for every business, but for me a ***virtual phone system*** was essential. We want our customers to feel they're important, and this formal answering system does this for us. Our phone system directs calls to specific members of our team, and it also transcribes voice mails and delivers them via e-mail. So, if I am unable to listen to my messages for any reason but I have access to e-mail, I can read my messages and respond immediately or forward them to someone who can. This investment was minimal for the return.

If you choose the right technological framework, you can have the added benefit of integration between these systems too. Together, they give you an executive dashboard from which to grow your business. Integrating your CRM system with your online accounting, mass e-mailing, and project management systems can make a significant impact on your business.

From my CRM dashboard alone, I am able to see the value of my clients and the value of my referral sources in dollars (thanks to integration with our online accounting software), which is really important as we analyze return on investment on campaign costs and time spent in networking opportunities.

In our bonus gift, we share with you the software selections we made after careful consideration-- and our experience of integrating them.

Invest in Training Your Support Staff

A last word on this section—invest in training your team. This may be nothing more than self-training via video tutorials, but be sure to set aside time for them to do that. The more they understand how to leverage your technical framework, the more value you'll get out of it in the long run.

Your Instant Insights...

- Implementing a technological framework increases organizational capacity and efficiency.

- Decide on and implement other solutions that may be extremely valuable while you're growing and building capacity, including project management, accounting, CRM, time tracking, social media management and scheduling, mass emailing software, and a virtual phone system.

- Prioritize and train your staff on the systems you've implemented.

Maintaining Your Thrive

As you come to the end of your forty-five-day journey, you may be feeling a little fatigued or even let down. This is completely normal. After running extremely hard and devoting every bit of your energy to reaching this goal, it's only normal to hit a wall once you finally get there.

What to Expect on Day 46 and the First Couple Weeks Thereafter

As you suddenly slow down, all the other things in your life that may have been set aside for the last forty-five days will slowly come back into focus. Now is a great time to take a step back and really acknowledge all that you've been able to accomplish in this time. You made it!

Look at your palm.
Place it on your back.
Give yourself a few pats.

Seriously, take this moment to really let that sink in. Feel it and enjoy it.

Time for Gratitude and Appreciation

Right after launching, I hit the wall and actually felt like I could have done more. A champion made a point of reminding me of all that I had accomplished. He made me write it all down. As I looked at the list, I thought, "Dang, I really did do a lot!" We can be hard on ourselves and lose sight of what we just accomplished. It's time for some gratitude and appreciation for getting through the last forty-five days and launching your business, and for all the people around you who were part of that process.

Make a Point of Thanking and Acknowledging Your Dream Team

Startup environments can feel a lot like the Wild West. The people you brought in during this process may feel insecure and uncertain now that the energy has slowed, and as a leader it's your responsibility to maintain the enthusiasm and momentum going forward. Acknowledge the wild ride you've all had together—the intensity and demand that these forty-five days had on the team and how great everyone did keeping up and delivering. Help them settle into a new operating routine while you all nurture and then harvest the seeds you planted as they begin to bear fruit and blossom.

Maintaining Stamina Post-Launch

So how do we maintain stamina in this post-launch phase? The best way to combat burnout is to create balance between your business and personal life. How do you do that? I started with:

- Sleep—lots of sleep
- Getting back to my healthy eating and exercising habits
- Reconnecting with the people I set aside temporarily in my personal life—my champions remain a very important part of my daily life.

Block time on your calendars to take care of yourself and guard it with your life. Self-care gives us the juice to thrive!

Exercise is extremely important for my own well-being, and it's something I completely neglected during my forty-five-day journey, so I formed a running group to get me back on track. Now, three days a week I have people to meet, and they hold me accountable. Whenever you involve someone else in a goal, it instantly creates accountability and improves your chances of accomplishing it.

This has proven successful for me with goals in all areas of my life.

Get a handle on your finances. It is essential to keep good records and maintain up-to-date books. You should seriously consider hiring a bookkeeper at this stage if you haven't already. You should also meet with your trusted advisor(s)—accountant, financial advisor, business consultant or coach. Let them help you analyze your numbers, and work with them to make necessary adjustments.

Farming begins to pay off between Days 45 and 90. You will begin to notice that some of the seeds you planted are beginning to bear fruit, and your farming is beginning to blossom!

Make another cut of people or networks who are not meeting your needs. You may also notice that some of the people that you invested time in or some of the networks you joined are no longer a good match. How do you know? You feel unwanted, criticized, exhausted or other negative feelings as a result of the time you invest with them. Be grateful that you are recognizing these signs, and return your focus to meeting other people and exploring other networks, which will enable you to meet your needs and continue to build your incredible network.

Remember, you are still in the very early stages of launching or relaunching your business. *It is a process of building, brick by brick.* Be patient as you continue this process. The farming will pay off.

Your Instant Insights...

- Pat yourself on your back and acknowledge all that you've accomplished in such a short period of time.

- Thank and acknowledge your amazing Dream Team.

- Get a handle on your finances, and watch as your farming turns into crops ready for harvest.

About the Author

Jodi Masters helps entrepreneurs live into their full potential and thrive As the CEO of Webvoice, Inc. she invents digital business opportunities for entrepreneurs by showing them specific ways to leverage the Internet and create digital versions of their product and services. As a result, they transform into more confident, successful entrepreneurs, thriving in their full potential.

For the past eighteen years, Masters has been reinventing and refining her expertise. The digitization of the world is creating incredible online networks. As a result the very nature of business branding is changing at a rapid pace. Masters is an expert at helping businesses to not only evolve in this new business landscape, but to thrive in it.

Masters understands that the entrepreneurial journey is never a straight line, and the power of having a champion by your side, who will brave your next adventure with you, is a transformative necessity. Masters embodies this belief and lives it daily. She truly is a champion for businesses who want to thrive.

She earned a BA from California State University, Long Beach, with a double major in sociology and international development. She studied for a year in Paris, attending Sorbonne, where she studied French language and culture.

Masters lives with her son, Frankie, on their yacht in a Southern California marina.

Connect with the Author

Website:
http://www.webvoice.com/

Email:
jodi@webvoice.com

Social Media:
Facebook: https://www.facebook.com/webvoiceinc/

LinkedIn: https://www.linkedin.com/in/webvoice

Twitter: @webvoice

Instagram: https://www.instagram.com/webvoice/

About Crescendo Publishing

Crescendo Publishing is a boutique-style, concierge VIP publishing company assisting entrepreneurs with writing, publishing, and promoting their books for the purposes of lead-generation and achieving global platform growth, then monetizing it for even more income opportunities.

Check out some of our latest best-selling AuthorPreneurs at http://CrescendoPublishing. com/new-authors/.

PUBLISHING

About the Instant Insights™ Book Series

The *Instant Insights™ Book Series* is a fact-only, short-read, book series written by EXPERTS in very specialized categories. These high-value, high-quality books can be produced in ONLY 6-8 weeks, from concept to launch, in BOTH PRINT & eBOOK Formats!

This book series is FOR YOU if:

- You are an expert in your niche or area of specialty

- You want to write a book to position yourself as an expert

- You want YOUR OWN book – NOT a chapter in someone else's book

- You want to have a book to give to people when you're speaking at events or simply networking

- You want to have it available quickly

- You don't have the time to invest in writing a 200-page full book

- You don't have a ton of money to invest in the production of a full book – editing, cover design, interior layout, best-seller promotion

- You don't have a ton of time to invest in finding quality contractors for the production of your book – editing, cover design, interior layout, best-seller promotion

For more information on how you can become an *Instant Insights™* author,
visit **www.InstantInsightsBooks.com**

More Books in the
Instant Insight™ Series

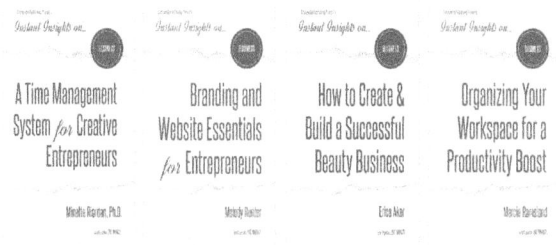

Instant Insights on...

A Time Management System *for* Creative Entrepreneurs

Minette Riordan, Ph.D.

Instant Insights on...

Branding and Website Essentials *for* Entrepreneurs

Melody Hunter

Instant Insights on...

How to Create & Build a Successful Beauty Business

Erica Akar

Instant Insights on...

Organizing Your Workspace for a Productivity Boost

Mimie Ransbland

Instant Insights on...

How to Be a Happy *&* Prosperous CEO

Joni Young

Instant Insights on...

Taking Your Business from Startup to Thrive in 45 Days

Jadi Masters

Instant Insights on...

7 Strategies *for* Raising Calm, Inspired, & Successful Children

Dr. Elaine Fogel Schneider, Ph.D.

Instant Insights on...

Creating a Solid, Lasting Connection with Your Kids

Dr. Vicki Panaccione

Instant Insights on...

12 Leadership Powers *for* Successful Women

Sylvia Becker-Hill

Instant Insights on...

MOTIVATION! Your Master Key to Success & Riches

Parviz Firouzgar

Instant Insights on...

PERFORMANCE POWER: Clarity, Confidence & Joy

Molly Mahoney

Instant Insights on...

Practical Natural Healing Tips for Vibrant Living

Lean Koenck